"Darling girl, when all else fails . . . join the circus."

UNKNOWN

In this skillful collection, images of the circus are central. The theme of these poems are balance: both literal, with ten antique carnival prose poems becoming the spine of the collection, as well as symbolic, with prose poems about women's stories/voices—balancing their growing/shrinking bodies and their ordinary/extraordinary lives. Funambulism– the art of walking the tight wire, writes courage into focus.

TIGHT
WIRE

Trace,
Wishing you balance. love. joy!

Fondly,

Kerry Gilbert

SFU Poems Sept. 2017

... prose poems ...

TIGHT WIRE

Kerry Gilbert

MOTHER TONGUE PUBLISHING LIMITED
Salt Spring Island B.C. Canada

MOTHER TONGUE PUBLISHING LIMITED
290 Fulford-Ganges Road, Salt Spring Island, B.C. v8k 2k6 Canada
www.mothertonguepublishing.com
Represented in North America by Heritage Group Distribution.

Book Design by Setareh Ashrafologhalai
Cover photos: *Female Acrobat Doing Splits*, 1940s; *Circus Midway Scene*, 1935,
    Photographer, Harry A. Atwell 1879–1957
Typefaces used are: Miller Old Style and Saloon Girl
Printed on Enviro Cream, 100% recycled
Printed and bound in Canada.

Mother Tongue Publishing gratefully acknowledges the assistance of the Province
of British Columbia through the B.C. Arts Council and we acknowledge the
support of the Canada Council for the Arts, which last year invested $157 million
in writing and publishing throughout Canada.

Nous remercions de son soutien le Conseil des Arts du Canada, qui a investi 157$
millions de dollars l'an dernier dans les lettres et l'édition à travers le Canada.

Library and Archives Canada Cataloguing in Publication

Gilbert, Kerry, author
 · Tight wire / Kerry Gilbert.

Poems.
ISBN 978-1-896949-53-6 (paperback)

 I. Title.

PS8613.I396T54 2016   C811'.6   C2016-901038-4

with love to my spokes: Natalie Appleton, Hannah Calder, Michelle Doege, Kristin Froneman, Karen Meyer and Laisha Rosnau

"A wheel would collapse if it wasn't for the spokes."

"She Rides"

EVALYN PARRY

funambulism. barefoot—no leather-soled slippers. her big and second toe cut deep in between by braided tight wire. no props—just

NO. 1

funambulism. barefoot—no leather-soled slippers. her big and
second toe cut deep in between by braided tight wire. no props—
just freehand. fully aware of her center of mass and of her core.
fully aware of the shallow tank of hammerheads below. circling.
fully aware of the ringmaster with the sawed-off shotgun pointed
at her back—aimed behind the curtains at her amateur heart—
and the black worn suitcase full of crumpled up cash at his feet.

the audience is unaware. they see beauty. sequins. perfection. poise.

to add to this spectacle, an assistant with a painted smile waits
at the side with her children. he will add them one by one while
she shifts her weight, and with her arms she sways side to side
with grace, even though blood drips to the tank from her feet.
she pushes against gravity because. because she loves her children
more than herself.

sweat cuts a new river through her clay makeup, but that too goes
unnoticed.

the jar is labeled "rat," printed with the thick black lines of a permanent marker, next to an empty jar labeled "pig." and even when the sun

researchers at the university of minnesota have grown a
beating heart in a jar—it sits on a white pressboard shelf next
to a series of metal mesh transom windows in a long, cool rect-
angular room. the jar is labeled "rat," printed with the thick
black lines of a permanent marker, next to an empty jar
labeled "pig."

and even when the sun is down and the fluorescent lights are
out, because everyone has gone home to warm conversations
and intimate food and sofa chairs that recline out and back
toward the bright glow of the television, it's there—the twitch
and pulse of a soft tissue chrysalis. a steady beat in an empty
shell—a dangling extension balanced precariously on the
edge of a soft, clear tube.

and, i'll tell you about the chapter i read in a thousand plateaus, while i folded tiny socks, while i scrubbed floor tiles, while i kneaded let me be your june cleaver—black-and-white cheek bones crisp and bold. i will splash some brazen pink on the dining room table, with orchids i grew in the greenhouse. the children will be: well-fed with freshly grown organic beefsteaks; well-bathed in lavender oil; well-loved and happily reading joseph campbell at their homeschool desks. i will chill your martini, dry—straight up, and sip on one too, to float smoothly into a sepia radiance.

you can tell me about your day, selling houses in this down-time—how it's a bear market.

and, i'll tell you about the chapter i read in *a thousand plateaus*, while i folded tiny socks, while i scrubbed floor tiles, while i kneaded whole wheat bread, while i made playdough, while i changed cloth diapers, while i answered emails, while i paid the bills, while i took the garbage out, while i taught the kids geometry, while i showered and applied artful face colour—*for you.*

and then i'll show you the chapter i wrote, in my next verse novel, while i grow orchids and stir martinis, dry.

it all starts the day he is born. he is so full of mucus he can't breathe on his back, so she holds him upright all night. fights sleep. feels it all starts the day he is born. he is so full of mucus he can't breathe on his back, so she holds him upright all night. fights sleep. feels the weight of his tiny breath against her skin and feels the first flutter of fear.

will he stop breathing? should we circumcise him? i heard a baby died after complications from his surgery. will he be allergic to peaches? should i wait another month before we try pablum? why isn't he pooping? does he have a fever? what's a normal temperature? what is this rash? will he fall down the stairs? i heard a toddler died after falling down a flight of stairs. will he always have a lisp? will he be mocked for it? is this cough serious? will they judge me for taking him to emergency? will he make it through his first day of kindergarten without tears? will he be taken by a broken human in a white van at recess? will he get bullied in grade eight? will a girl break his heart? will he drive drunk? will he experiment with drugs? will he experiment with sex? will he experiment with sex and drugs, drunk? will he be happy? will he be a good father? will he get enough sleep with a new baby? will he work too much, to afford high rent in a dark moldy basement suite? will she love him?

the exact second the steel i-beam falls off the truck and splits his head, across the country, her stomach splits open and out fly 434 glasswing butterflies—one for every month he was alive.

they climb each other and bend and flex into a fleshy sculpture. they morph into one another until three become one. legs become arms

NO. 2

cirque—contortionism. bodies tied in a knot.

three faux-naked mongolian sisters, trained to contort since
they were five, because they come from a long line of naturally
flexible women. and their father makes a living off their flex-
ibility. as their coach, he has them train at least eight hours
a day.

they climb each other and bend and flex into a fleshy sculpture. they morph into one another until three become one.
legs become arms. buttocks become breasts. round softness
becomes sharp art angles. they become a three-headed still
life, with one synchronized exhale for a breath. even their
smiles solidify.

the audience gasps in awe at the beautiful, beautiful pain.

my clunky heart grasps back against my rib cage toward them. squeezes flat until i have to pull over and open the car door for air. i focus

it's time to leave. time to say goodbye. six tiny hands wave
wildly through the window—growing small through the side-
view mirror. my clunky heart grasps back against my rib cage
toward them. squeezes flat until i have to pull over and open
the car door for air.

i focus on the lines on the road. focus on the cars passing
by—one by one. focus on sipping cold coffee. focus on the
slow, methodical beat of a song played on repeat. focus on the
woman's automatic navigation voice, directing me away. away.
away. *prepare to turn right in 100 meters. turn. right. now.*
prepare to turn left in 20 meters. turn. left. now. drive straight.
drive away from your family, you selfish courtesan. and i am.
and i do.

and it isn't until i'm out of the trenched valley, driving straight
through cloud-speckled farmland that the weight shifts
forward and pushes towards the front of my rib cage. i drive
straight and fast between the beautifully treacherous thighs
of the rocky mountains.

you. have reached your destination.

her red housecoat open pond-shaped around her naked body. full of chills but her arms cannot move to warm her. full of words but

how does a forty-two-year-old woman have a stroke? it
happens—at 8:24 on a thursday morning. a dust cloud still
visible from the school bus—already gone with the three children whose backpacks are carefully packed, whose bodies are
tastefully clothed, teeth and hair brushed and cheeks kissed
at least twice each. the coffee pot light blares red. still hot and
a quarter full—even after making him a cup before his shower
and a cup to go.

before it's her turn to make her own and shower. before work
and meetings and deadlines, she falls to the floor—her red
housecoat open pond-shaped around her naked body. full of
chills, but her arms cannot move to warm her. full of words,
but her mouth cannot move to speak.

she lies like this until 3:05 when the children enter through
the kitchen door.

the ambulance blares red and kicks up a dust cloud—for the
first time she sees beautiful, slow connections, but cannot say
what they are.

in the front of a small square room with only one window and full of familiar strangers, she stands in tree pose—roots planted from toes

in the front of a small square room with only one window
and full of familiar strangers, she stands in tree pose—roots
planted from toes on an imaginary tightrope. *lift your arms
and be whatever kind of tree you want to be.* she finds the edge
of an old willow, sways slightly, breathes deeply in and out
and in and out. and then comes out of it—muscles twitch to
compensate balance. steps her right leg directly back behind
the left, squats into battle pose and lifts her arms up high—
warrior one. feels the strength and the wobble. feels the edge
of an old heavy sword. feels the rope tighten under her feet.

*now, put your arms behind your back, lace your fingers
together and push your chest forward. be a warrior with
your heart open—strong, but soft.*

she woke trapped in this new skin—a vine that noosed around her neck then shot deep-coloured roses across her face. family got angry

NO. 3

the tattooed woman started out with only one tattoo—a simple
rose vine cuff around her ankle—but it grew. the vine spread
and blossomed up her leg and thigh and waist over one breast,
down her arm and cuffed around her wrist. and while she slept,
her wrists tied together as it crept up the other arm and down
the other side of her body. she woke trapped in this new skin—
a vine that noosed around her neck then shot deep-coloured
roses across her face.

family got angry—*how could this happen to you.* friends
stopped looking in her eyes, and so she joins the circus. poses
mostly naked. strangers marvel at the deep ink that took over
her body, and they wonder, what kind of girl was she.

someone who saw the whole thing from the shadows of her kitchen—houses so close that secrets couldn't hide—she called the police

*i know that he hit you. i know that there was screaming and
breaking and sirens.*

but the drinking was only anecdotal for us. small memories,
like small ears and eyes and mouths, of both of you too drunk.
messy parents. broken parents. and you finally split after that.
he flew to southeast asia to find a younger version of you. and
you—you never really got up. *broken parent.* never spoke a
word to anyone except to someone who knew you very well.
someone who saw the whole thing from the shadows of her
kitchen—houses so close that secrets couldn't hide—she called
the police. she also called me, but told me not to tell.

i know that he hit you.

i have always known, but my mouth shrank so small until all
that is left are tiny, insignificant gestures. just the way you
want it.

later he takes off her top hat. unpins her braided hair. it falls in a straight line down the center of her back. he takes off her long white gloves

dressage—french for "training." horse ballet. she adds pressure
with her inner thighs and resists the thick dark muscles of her
horse. it's a test. the animal's *natural athletic ability and will-
ingness to perform*. she shifts her weight and gently pulls the
braided mane. it responds and bends into a perfect bow. head
tucked down. one front leg bent in. the other extended. brown
eyes down—close to the ground. elegant. *good girl. good girl.*

later he takes off her top hat. unpins her braided hair. it falls
in a straight line down the center of her back. he takes off her
long white gloves and tall black boots. takes off her stretch
pants but leaves the black blazer on—undone. he pushes her
into position and pulls her braid back as the thick muscles in
his bum tense. she bends into a perfect bow. head tucked down.
elegant. eyes down—close to the ground. *good girl. good girl.*

he has her climb the first part of the fence then he lifts her over. lets her go in first and climbs in after. he can't hurt. at first, his hairy lips she's five and school makes her have glasswing butterflies in her belly. at recess the teacher always pushes her out and out and out. she finds the furthest corner of the field, where two edges of the fence meet and she can watch the children play with her back to the horses in the neighbor's yard. horses can't hurt. she feeds them her mini carrots sometimes, and their hairy lips tickle her hand.

one day in february, there is an igloo snow fort on the other side of the fence, like the kind her brother makes in their back-yard. she sticks her fingers through the fence to try and reach it, but it's too far away. she pulls a twig from the weeping willow in the schoolyard and sticks it through to touch.

a man's voice comes from inside. *you like my horses?* she drops the twig. she has been taught to be polite to adults. *yes sir.* he crawls out from the fort and stands up next to the fence. he's shorter than her daddy. *would you like to touch it?*

yes sir. he has her climb the first part of the fence then he lifts her over. lets her go in first and climbs in after. he can't hurt. at first, his hairy lips tickle.

raunchy music begins. so do spits and whistles. the cage is raised, not even subtly, by the groan of an old splayed rope, being pulled in the

NO. 4

burlesque—cirque style—on a black, black stage, a sudden
white light creates a perfect circle. in the center of the circle
is a copper-coloured cage big enough to fit a small child. the
cage is white feather full.

raunchy music begins. so do spits and whistles. the cage is
raised, not even subtly, by the groan of an old splayed rope,
being pulled in the rafters by the grunt of an old damp man.

the feathers unfurl to show a pale, curvy naked woman—
marilynesque—crouched to the ground. as she slowly
rises—seductively—she spreads her arms wide, feather tips
stretch past the boundaries of the light into the darkness. she
has sequined shells pasted to her nipples and to her hairless
crotch. they catch fragments of light as she moves like falling
water, until the music stops.

then she folds the feathers in and crouches down still, until
the cage covers her once again and the stage goes black, black.

so she closes her mouth tight and holds her breath in and crosses her legs closed and lays on her back and feels the growing weight of her

she's so full of life, they need to put a stitch in her cervix so
it doesn't fall out too soon. the lungs to her thoughts need to
develop. the stomach be able to digest. the mouth able to latch.
the heart able to pump. she's so full of love, she needs to stay
horizontal. keep her legs slightly above her heart—so it doesn't
fall out. she's so full of hope, they put her on progesterone, to
strengthen the chances.

so she closes her mouth tight and holds her breath in and
crosses her legs closed and lays on her back and feels the
growing weight of her belly balance precariously between in
and out.

and he eternalizes her in this way, heavy lead on pressed paper,
femme nue couchée —she sits perfectly while he sketches her
still over the next four months.

he gives her the fruit. she eats it too fast, right to the core. skips what's left across the shore of kalamalka. where it sinks a weeping willow in a twist, he gives her the fruit. she eats it too fast, right to the core. skips what's left across the shore of kalamalka. where it sinks a weeping willow grows. as penance, he births the twins, like a seahorse. she becomes a cardiologist, specializes in children's health. makes four hundred thousand per year. they live happily in a glass house on the lake. he makes beautiful miniature wooden toys. or,

he gives her the fruit. she eats it too fast, right to the core. skips what's left across the shore of kalamalka. where it sinks a weeping willow grows—but this time, the apple is full of worms.

once in her stomach, they turn and tunnel through her body. guilt burrows entire empty hollows between the thick layers of flesh, until she becomes a light wooden shell—a bright blue and yellow and red and pink and white ukrainian nesting doll on the outside with bigger and smaller, better and worse versions of her neatly tucked in.

the clouds are the shape of a woman. head thrown back. mouth wide open—silently screaming. she knows she is done. she knows. she in the bath, her body becomes liquid. listens to the drip. drip. drip. of water. listens to a wasp stuck in between the screen and window. looks past that, out at the sky. searches piles of cumulous. realizes that she's barely breathing—just shallow ripple breaths that hardly move the water. realizes she's been like this for a while.

the dark clouds move slow like a scene from *wings of desire*— marion on her trapeze. she closes her eyes.

full   breath   in,   full   breath   out

when she opens them, the clouds are the shape of a woman. head thrown back. mouth wide open—silently screaming. she knows she is done. she knows. *she has known for a while.*

in the reflection of unmoving water, the head slowly dissipates and forms a rudimentary heart.

muscle is a masculine word, and her back, when she flexes like a man, is pure muscle—like the thigh of a galloping stallion. she can bench

NO. 5

strongwoman—muscle is a masculine word, and her back,
when she flexes like a man, is pure muscle—like the thigh of
a galloping stallion. she can bench press 300 pounds. she can
bend steel bars. she can resist the pull of multiple horses. she
can pick up three or four men at one time. she has less than 4%
body fat—to the point that she can no longer conceive. but she
doesn't need to—the circus is her family now. the men who do
not look her in the eye. the women who do—she collects their
eyeballs in jars tucked away on deep shelves in her long silver
trailer. she names every last one.

she begins to peel, slow and methodical. it has to be just right. when completely off, she pulls and stretches and pins each edge perfectly

with a tiny scalpel, she carefully cuts the skin just underneath
her blouse line. down the sides to her hips. to her ankles.
around and up her inner thighs—both sides. not her face. not
her hands. not her feet. when the cuts are symmetrical and
thorough, she begins to peel, slow and methodical. it has to
be just right. when completely off, she pulls and stretches and
pins each edge perfectly to a sapling tanning frame. she lights
it from behind with soft spotlights and stands in the far corner.

people come from all around to see her art. they debate over
what it is. awe over the translucent stretch marks. speculate
that the nipples *are marks painted to show a stained patriar-
chal society.* they touch it gently, hoping the texture will offer
clues to what it is. no one admits they do not know. then they
shake her hand, framed delicately by a tiny pearl bracelet and
ivory blouse, they kiss her on the cheek and say *amazing—
how—do you do it?*

when she balances precariously, with at least seven tubes coming out of her body to let the septic out, she can't help thinking that birth

she didn't want to have a hysterectomy, but her heavy uterus
said otherwise—all the women on her mother's side end up
with full uteruses after childbirth, like phantom pregnancies—
it will be okay—they say—*common procedure, nothing to it.*

maybe the leading surgeon didn't have sex that morning, and
the site of her exposed fallopian tubes made him flush a little;
or maybe he's going through his second divorce and has to sign
the paperwork after this *little procedure*; or maybe, just maybe,
he found out the news that he is going to be a father for the first
time—and in his preoccupation, with a slight quiver of hand,
his knife enters her bowel intimately. not noticing, he sews her
back up. they don't understand it has happened until she goes
into shock.

and when she balances precariously, with at least seven tubes
coming out of her body to let the septic out, she can't help
thinking that birth and death are the same thing—*petite mort*—
and that somehow she knew it all along.

i'm deep in the rockies, and this is where she slowly evolved from a crisp, thin black-and-white photo, to a full-fleshed woman. until she i think my nana wants to be in here too. i'm deep in the rockies, and this is where she slowly evolved from a crisp, thin black-and-white photo, to a full-fleshed woman. until she slowly disintegrated and became turquoise dust that settled as silt at the bottom of lake o'hara.

she told me in those days before, when there were still fragments of her left, that she'd come back as a crow—*like papa did*. sure enough, the morning she died, two flew side by side in front of my bay window. sure enough, as i was driving toward banff, she flew next to me for at least a mile.

so here you go, nana—beautiful feathered mother of mothers— you are here at the heart of it.

the kind that sucks on a springy auburn curl while carefully pushing peas with her finger to a designated spot on her plate—leaving the

NO. 6

the 737-pound woman on display was a slender child—the
kind that sucks on a springy auburn curl while carefully
pushing peas with her finger to a designated spot on her
plate—leaving the mashed potatoes untouched—mount vesu-
vius heavy with thick sauce. but then, when she was five, she
witnessed a girl crawl into a backyard snow fort with a man
at recess. and in the swiftest of moments, faster than melting
butter on warm bread, she ate the child all up—wiping the last
curl from her drippy wet mouth before anyone could guess
what had happened. and as the years passed, she grew with
different versions of the same girl over and over and over until
now, up on a dimly lit stage, she sits on an ornate tapestry sofa,
in a soft pink baby doll dress—her curls pinned too high with a
doubled-up silk ribbon.

she is so full of love she can't breathe. feels like she could run out of this heavy perfect house, go straight to the airport, in her new silk after seven years, two months and three days of trying to conceive, the woman sits in the dark—empty wombed—at midnight and searches the computer for babies: from the ukraine, from china, from south africa. at the start, her husband had said he didn't want to adopt; he feared he wouldn't love the child as much as his own. the thought sits on her—she is so full of love she can't breathe. feels like she could run out of this heavy perfect house, go straight to the airport, in her new silk butterfly nightgown, board a plane maniacally— head thrown back. mouth wide open—go pluck a baby out of an orphanage and run.

what happens if there is no mother? no vaginal birth. no suckle at the breast—just the synthetic kind. no skin on skin contact. no kisses

what happens if there is no mother? no vaginal birth. no suckle
at the breast—just the synthetic kind. no skin on skin contact.
no kisses on broken bones and stitches and scabs. no soft
fingers that erase salt tears. no tellers of fantastical tales that
help children sleep through the night.

will there be a sense of isolation? levels of anxiety on the rise?
depression in small children? the inability to empathize with
others? fear?

or, like darwin's finches, will fathers' hands grow softer—less
calloused to compensate. and will their fine-haired arms
encircle our children until they are whole again.

she plants her thick mother legs deep into the sand—a declaration—a conversation with the sea. water rolls over and over and over her the sea of cortez—a ruthless sea—it licks at their ankles, licks at their calves, licks at their knees and whips out their feet with a vicious tongue until they are gone. a mother watches her daughter float down and away. she swims with every sinew—fast—hard—pushes like birth. arms and hands and fingers stretch out to catch her—*my baby*

the waves pull her child out further and further into a half sun—*gone*. she swims with every memory of her baby calling—*m o m m o m m o m*—with the feeling of a heartbeat on her bare skin for the first time. she swims with salt water scratching against her skin. until she can't tell the difference between up and down and here and there—she can't see her daughter's silhouette any more—she can't see the half sun—*they are gone.*

she plants her thick mother legs deep into the sand—a declaration—a conversation with the sea. water rolls over and over and over her, and she pushes back and back and back. *this— is—not— over!*

they pick up her thick seaweed body and bring her to shore. sit her in the sand next to her exhausted daughter—already saved.

man with the greasy fingers pressed on the button with a grotesque smile, and the deep, deep shadows that only an adult could recognize

NO. 7

carnival carousal—ornate detail framed by white lights. horses
with painted eyes and stilted breath. and a five-year-old girl—
too ambivalent, too polite to question the queasiness, the up
and downedness, the twisting tinny music, the mirrors gliding
by faster and faster, the man with the greasy fingers pressed on
the button with a grotesque smile, and the deep, deep shadows
that only an adult could recognize.

thirty years later, she still can't seem to lift her stubborn feet
off that familiar glide—the love/hate relationship of it all—the
repetition has left dark grooves in the ground. and besides, she
knows the routine of this song, every minute movement of it,
by heart.

corner of her windshield a black alarm clock falls from the sky and leaves a small glass dent—the kind that fractures and spreads over time it happens on a tuesday morning. on the drive to work. small drops of rain smudge the window—not enough to turn the wipers on. she keeps driving. it picks up. picks up. picks up. soon full torrential drops drop. wipers wipe wildly. she strains to see ahead but keeps driving—she is late for work.

in the right hand corner of her windshield, a black alarm clock falls from the sky and leaves a small glass dent—the kind that fractures and spreads over time. before she can react, a mobile phone hits the middle of the hood and spirals over top of the car. then a stainless steel coffee pot. a laptop. a glass paper-weight with an exclamation mark on it. she stops, diagonal in the middle of things.

all around her, items fall from the sky. a toaster oven—the kind big enough to fit a 12" pizza. a 52" lcd flat screen. a wrought iron coatrack. a doghouse. an automatic outdoor pool cover. a front-loading washer and drier. a quad. cross-country skis. a vacuum cleaner. a bathtub—with gold-crusted claw legs. a king-size bed—with 100% egyptian cotton sheets. a black leather back massage chair. dozens and dozens of jimmy choos.

a bmw lands upside down ten feet in front of her. a house spirals smoothly from the sky and lands on the car. a stained coffee mug lands perfectly upright on the hood in front of her. it says *don't mess with me—i'm the mom.*

to the sound of heavy thuds on the roof of the car, the mug slowly, slowly begins to collect rain water.

and when she is beyond tired and the baby finally falls, still attached by the lifeline, and sinks to the bottom of the pool, she is in awe it is so important to her that her first birth be *all natural*. she spends months reiterating her birth plan. no drugs. no episiotomy. no birth in a bed. water. it has to be in water. she hires a doula—despite her mother's advice for a well-trained doctor. she reads books. she watches videos. she talks to other women about their experiences. she feels, *ready*.

when it's time, she is surprised by the inner conflict—the protagonist/antagonist of it all. she isn't ready for the world to mute but not freeze—for the overwhelming desire for drugs. for the quickness versus slowness of things. for the out-of-controll-ness of it all.

and when she is beyond tired and the baby finally falls, still attached by the lifeline, and sinks to the bottom of the pool, she is in awe that it is in fact natural. she stares at the tiny rippled body with fine floating hair. its dark eyes open, staring straight up—barely blinking—such a bloated understanding between mother and child. so much so, she forgets to pick it up.

trapped in the bed with no shadows to hide under because she is chained beneath the sway of a 110-watt light bulb that is her only sun

for ten years she is trapped in the room with no windows—
trapped in the house where sound absorbs into cool white
walls—trapped in the bed with no shadows to hide under
because she is chained beneath the sway of a 110-watt light
bulb that is her only sun.

she can't breathe under the fleshy weight of him.

but, what can i do about it? i write him off of her. i write him
out of the room. out of the house. out of the suburb. out of this
decade. back to the schoolyard. lay him on the crusty snow,
cut open his chest and transplant his heart with one that i've
grown in a jar.

these women trapped in a hall of mirrors—flat and glossy. tall and slender. short and fat. convex and concave—in and out and in and out

NO. 8

these voices. their voices. their faces.

these women trapped in a hall of mirrors—flat and glossy. tall
and slender. short and fat. convex and concave—in and out and
in and out. their mouths slightly open, but in a reverse echo,
sound comes from another room, from another mouth. it's a
maze, it's a maze, it's a maze from every angle.

these voices. their voices. their faces.

the haunting sound of them running through glass.

always polite, i apologize as a thousand mirrored versions of
myself scatter to the floor.

her skin cracks deep fissures. when she opens her red housecoat, her breasts tumble off. she tries to say something, but her mouth is arid it starts fairly subtle, fairly insignificant, while they watch a documentary about snakes in south america. the feeling of dread in her stomach starts to feel heavier—more solid. her always-stiff shoulders start to feel even more so. muscles contract and squeeze in on themselves until it's difficult to breathe. the thuds of her heart echo, dry. she listens. *can they hear it too?* she waits until a commercial and then quietly pushes the weight of her body off the couch. as she walks towards the bathroom, fine dust falls to the floor—goes unnoticed. in front of the full length mirror, behind locked doors, she sees it.

she's turned to clay.

as she leans in closer to look, her skin cracks deep fissures. when she opens her red housecoat, her breasts tumble off. she tries to say something, but her mouth is arid as a canyon. her ears crumble, her shoulders erode, her hips shrink. tears cut a new river as her landscape silently shakes and echoes. with her stone fingers, she spreads pooled moisture over her face. she reshapes her ears. she reshapes perfect/imperfect breasts and hips and smooths the skin until all the tears are absorbed. she tries out a smile. closes her housecoat, flushes the toilet for effect, and walks smoothly back to the couch.

one of her daughters sits close and holds her soft, malleable hand.

that she could see me watching her cry through the crack of the mostly closed bathroom door. me wedged between the door and the wall

i can't get the image of my always-stoic mother out of my head—
bent over the linoleum floor in tears the day we planted cedars
in the backyard. i was scared it was because i threw shavings at
my brothers or that she could see me watching her cry through
the crack of the mostly closed bathroom door. me wedged
between the door and the wall.

i get it now. the weight. the worry. the inconsistencies. the
contradictions. the double standards. the love. the hate. the
balancing. the balancing. the balancing. the imbalances. and
i wish, i wish more than anything i could go back to that day,
push open the door and help a broken woman up.

the black-and-white scene play out while perched angel high on a trapeze swing in the corner of the room. legs pump for momentum while birthing she can't see colour. watches the black-and-white scene play out while perched angel high on a trapeze swing in the corner of the room. legs pump for momentum. she floats up and away and fights with every sinew—fast, hard. to be in two places at once.

when you feel like you've pushed as hard as you can, push harder

and just when she thinks there is no more strength, life slips out. for the first time, she sees beautiful, slow connections—dark petals painted between light thighs. a baby that comes out grey and doesn't scream. they cut it free, fast and take it. as she sits up to see, the room goes silent and slow with quick white flashes of light—feathered life photos stuck to thick black paper.

finally the baby girl screams, and the whole room bursts into colour. the worried pink in the doctor's cheeks, the bloodstains on the white sheets, the colour that starts from her lips and spreads over her entire body, down to her little complicated splayed fingers and toes.

lastly he takes out a machete. men gasp their smoke in, hold it there while he one, two, three aims in the air then lets it spiral until it lands

NO. 9

impalement art—gypsy target girl, attached to a wooden
wheel of death by chain cuffs on her wrists and ankles,
revealing to the crowd the shadows of her exposed cleavage
and inner thighs. a masked man spins the rustic wheel,
causing the dangling rope of a 110-volt bulb to sway—the only
light in the darkened room—casting grotesque figures on the
four walls. he takes ten paces back, looks at the crowd of men
smoking cigars—wide-eyed—and throws the first little knife,
while watching smoke accumulate like dark clouds above their
heads. it lands with a hollow thud to the left of her heart. in
a succession of speed, while she continues to turn and turn
and turn—a rusty sound resonates—he chooses from a wicker
basket, knives of varying size as he throws and outlines her
body perfectly in steel. lastly he takes out a machete. men
gasp their smoke in, hold it there while he *one, two, three* aims
in the air then lets it spiral until it lands *thud*, right between
her legs.

smoke is exhaled and so is the excited murmur of men.

with a tiny scalpel, she slowly cuts a perfect dividing line between her breasts. then crosses the t with the same trajectory that he did with guilt is making her heart sluggish.

with a tiny scalpel, she slowly cuts a perfect dividing line
between her breasts. then crosses the t with the same trajectory that he did with his lips the first time he saw them,
when he kissed across to each nipple and claimed them by
naming them.

she carefully peels back from the center meeting point, four
half triangles of fresh under-skin finally exposed. she does the
same to the next layer and the next—a lotus blooming from
blood between her breasts—until she reaches the heart.

she pulls it out carefully and puts it on the kitchen table.
dissects it into quarters skillfully—with as much precision
as she takes to sew halloween costumes. teach hemingway's
iceberg theory. make love. write a poem.

she wraps up each section in pressed tissue paper, puts them
in four empty glass jars, and saves them for later.

she smells the salt in the air and listens to the lap. lap. lap. of the liquid at her toes. crows circle crabs hidden under rocks. i hold her hand she squats, barefoot, on the pebbles of a westcoast beach, the sound of whales breeching in the distance as she bares down.

her husband tries to feed her ice chips. the doctors talk in hushed tones about what they are going to do with the dead baby.

she smells the salt in the air and listens to the lap. lap. lap. of the liquid at her toes. crows circle crabs hidden under rocks.

i hold her hand, but i don't think she knows i am here. i hold the baby for a moment, swaddled like a proper newborn, before they take him away.

she slowly stands and walks away from us all, away. away. down the most beautiful long wet pebbled beach i have ever seen.

of wrapping her blues and blacks with a soft white silk, over the curves of her ins and her outs, over the hollow of her mouth and her eyes what are the implications: when she isn't so brilliant—colours now muted, lines fractured, glass wings opaque—of wrapping her blues and blacks with a soft white silk, over the curves of her ins and her outs, over the hollow of her mouth and her eyes and her ears. for when she chooses this quiet instead of flight.

a second chrysalis—leaving babies to grow themselves for a while—leaving the world to twist haphazardly on its axis— leaving predators out and keeping the heart in—to echo a steady beat in this new shell—a dangling extension balanced precariously on the edge of a soft, green leaf.

she cuts the tightrope with the squeak of rusty scissors. feels the instant weight of air

NO. 10

in an act of pain so fundamentally ignored—only the
blood from her toes speaks it—she cuts the tightrope with
the squeak of rusty scissors. feels the instant weight of air
beneath her and the whoosh of not standing still.

the carousal's music stops as horses glide to a slow. the
mongolian sisters tumble to the floor. the fat woman gasps
a guttural gasp.

in the days and weeks that follow, the ground is littered
with bent ticket stubs and stale popcorn. there is the
phantom noise of crowds and the fading footprints in
dust of those who came to enjoy the show.

for now

it is over.

ACKNOWLEDGEMENTS

It is with deep gratitude that I thank the following places/people for their inspiration, their support and their guidance:

Thank you to BC Arts Council and Banff Arts Centre for helping artists be artists.

Thank you to Okanagan College for the time and space to honor my craft. Special thanks to John Lent, Craig McLuckie, Alix Hawley and Kevin McPherson for letting me talk out writing over the years.

Also I'd like to whole heartedly thank Mona Fertig for believing in me and in this manuscript. Your kindness is beautiful and is appreciated.

I would also like to thank Judith Brand for your meticulous editing and Setareh Ashrafologhalai for your beautiful design.

I have deep gratitude to my writers group: Natalie Appleton, Hannah Calder, Michelle Doege, Kristin Froneman, Karen Meyer and Laisha Rosnau. You each inspire me beyond words.

To all of my family who are friends and friends who are family—especially Marty, Avery, Kiera and Evan who have the biggest chunk of my love.

BIOGRAPHY

KERRY GILBERT grew up in the Okanagan. She has lived on
Vancouver Island, in South Korea, and in Australia. She now
lives back in the valley, where she teaches at Okanagan College
and raises her three children. Her first book, (kerplnk): a verse
novel of development, was published in 2005.